The Insanity Defense

CRIME, JUSTICE, AND PUNISHMENT

The Insanity Defense

Richard Worth

Austin Sarat, GENERAL EDITOR

CHELSEA HOUSE PUBLISHERS
Philadelphia

Frontispiece: *The world of the mentally ill, difficult for laypersons to comprehend, also presents special problems for the legal system.*

Chelsea House Publishers

Editor in Chief Sally Cheney
Production Manager Pamela Loos
Art Director Sara Davis
Director of Photography Judy L. Hasday
Managing Editor James D. Gallagher
Senior Production Editor J. Christopher Higgins

Staff for THE INSANITY DEFENSE

Senior Editor John Ziff
Associate Art Director/Designer Takeshi Takahashi
Picture Researcher Patricia Burns
Cover Designer Takeshi Takahashi

3 5 7 9 8 6 4 2

The Chelsea House World Wide Web address is
http://www.chelseahouse.com

Library of Congress Cataloging-in-Publication Data

Worth, Richard.
The insanity defense / Richard Worth.
  p. cm. — (Crime, justice, and punishment)
Includes bibliographical references and index.

ISBN 0-7910-4294-4 (hc)

1. Insanity—Jurisprudence—United States—Juvenile literature. 2. Criminal liability—United
States—Juvenile literature. [1. Insanity—Jurisprudence. 2. Law.] I. Title. II. Series.

KF9242.Z9 W67 2000
345.73'04—dc21
00-040507

Contents

CRIME, JUSTICE, AND PUNISHMENT

Fears and Fascinations:

An Introduction to Crime, Justice, and Punishment

By Austin Sarat

We live with crime and images of crime all around us. Crime evokes in most of us a deep aversion, a feeling of profound vulnerability, but it also evokes an equally deep fascination. Today, in major American cities the fear of crime is a major fact of life, some would say a disproportionate response to the realities of crime. Yet the fear of crime is real, palpable in the quickened steps and furtive glances of people walking down darkened streets. At the same time, we eagerly follow crime stories on television and in movies. We watch with a "who done it" curiosity, eager to see the illicit deed done, the investigation undertaken, the miscreant brought to justice and given his just deserts. On the streets the presence of crime is a reminder of our own vulnerability and the precariousness of our taken-for-granted rights and freedoms. On television and in the movies the crime story gives us a chance to probe our own darker motives, to ask "Is there a criminal within?" as well as to feel the collective satisfaction of seeing justice done.

Fear and fascination, these two poles of our engagement with crime, are, of course, only part of the story. Crime is, after all, a major social and legal problem, not just an issue of our individual psychology. Politicians today use our fear of, and fascination with, crime for political advantage. How we respond to crime, as well as to the political uses of the crime issue, tells us a lot about who we are as a people as well as what we value and what we tolerate. Is our response compassionate or severe? Do we seek to understand or to punish, to enact an angry vengeance or to rehabilitate and welcome the criminal back into our midst? The CRIME, JUSTICE, AND PUNISHMENT series is designed to explore these themes, to ask why we are fearful and fascinated, to probe the meanings and motivations of crimes and criminals and of our responses to them, and, finally, to ask what we can learn about ourselves and the society in which we live by examining our responses to crime.

Crime is always a challenge to the prevailing normative order and a test of the values and commitments of law-abiding people. It is sometimes a Raskolnikov-like act of defiance, an assertion of the unwillingness of some to live according to the rules of conduct laid out by organized society. In this sense, crime marks the limits of the law and reminds us of law's all-too-regular failures. Yet sometimes there is more desperation than defiance in criminal acts; sometimes they signal a deep pathology or need in the criminal. To confront crime is thus also to come face-to-face with the reality of social difference, of class privilege and extreme deprivation, of race and racism, of children neglected, abandoned, or abused whose response is to enact on others what they have experienced themselves. And occasionally crime, or what is labeled a criminal act, represents a call for justice, an appeal to a higher moral order against the inadequacies of existing law.

Figuring out the meaning of crime and the motivations of criminals and whether crime arises from defiance, desperation, or the appeal for justice is never an easy task. The motivations and meanings of crime are as varied as are the persons who engage in criminal conduct. They are as mysterious as any of the mysteries of the human soul. Yet the desire to know the secrets of crime and the criminal is a strong one, for in that knowledge may lie one step on the road to protection, if not an assurance of one's own personal safety. Nonetheless, as strong as that desire may be, there is no available technology that can allow us to know the whys of crime with much confidence, let alone a scientific certainty. We can, however, capture something about crime by studying the defiance, desperation, and quest for justice that may be associated with it. Books in the Crime, Justice, and Punishment series will take up that challenge. They tell stories of crime and criminals, some famous, most not, some glamorous and exciting, most mundane and commonplace.

This series will, in addition, take a sober look at American criminal justice, at the procedures through which we investigate crimes and identify criminals, at the institutions in which innocence or guilt is determined. In these procedures and institutions we confront the thrill of the chase as well as the challenge of protecting the rights of those who defy our laws. It is through the efficiency and dedication of law enforcement that we might capture the criminal; it is in the rare instances of their corruption or brutality that we feel perhaps our deepest betrayal. Police, prosecutors, defense lawyers, judges, and jurors administer criminal justice and in their daily actions give substance to the guarantees of the Bill of Rights. What is an adversarial system of justice? How does it work? Why do we have it? Books in the Crime, Justice, and Punishment series will examine the thrill of the chase as we seek to capture the criminal. They will also reveal the drama and majesty of the criminal trial as well as the day-to-day reality of a criminal justice system in which trials are the exception and negotiated pleas of guilty are the rule.

When the trial is over or the plea has been entered, when we have separated the innocent from the guilty, the moment of punishment has arrived. The injunction to punish the guilty, to respond to pain inflicted by inflicting pain, is as old as civilization itself. "An eye for an eye and a tooth for a tooth" is a biblical reminder that punishment must measure pain for pain. But our response to the criminal must be better than and different from the crime itself. The biblical admonition, along with the constitutional prohibition of "cruel and unusual punishment," signals that we seek to punish justly and to be just not only in the determination of who can and should be punished, but in how we punish as well. But neither reminder tells us what to do with the wrongdoer. Do we rape the rapist, or burn the home of the arsonist? Surely justice and decency say no. But, if not, then how can and should we punish? In a world in which punishment is neither identical to the crime nor an automatic response to it, choices must be made and we must make them. Books in the CRIME, JUSTICE, AND PUNISHMENT series will examine those choices and the practices, and politics, of punishment. How do we punish and why do we punish as we do? What can we learn about the rationality and appropriateness of today's responses to crime by examining our past and its responses? What works? Is there, and can there be, a just measure of pain?

CRIME, JUSTICE, AND PUNISHMENT brings together books on some of the great themes of human social life. The books in this series capture our fear and fascination with crime and examine our responses to it. They remind us of the deadly seriousness of these subjects. They bring together themes in law, literature, and popular culture to challenge us to think again, to think anew, about subjects that go to the heart of who we are and how we can and will live together.

*   *   *   *   *

The insanity defense, which is often misunderstood, generates quite a bit of controversy. While many people think that the insanity defense is frequently used, the truth is that the defense is rarely raised and even more rarely successful. And, when it is successful, the defendant generally isn't released outright but faces confinement in a mental hospital. Part of the misunderstanding and controversy surrounding the insanity defense arises because of its use in high-profile cases, such as the trial of John Hinckley for the attempted assassination of President Ronald Reagan. In addition, while insanity sounds like a psychological term, the legal definition of insanity traditionally has not followed the psychological meaning.

Misunderstanding and controversy would seem to call for a calm and balanced assessment of the place of the insanity defense in our criminal justice system. This is exactly what *The Insanity Defense* provides. Richard Worth presents a fine overview of the most pressing issues with respect to this legal concept. He provides a useful historical summary of the origins and development of the insanity defense as well as an insightful treatment of recent reform efforts. Because it revolves around the analysis of celebrated cases in which the insanity defense has played an important role, the book offers unusually engaging reading. The treatment of John Hinckley provides a very useful window onto the difficulties and uncertainties in ascertaining who is insane. *The Insanity Defense* also provides a riveting analysis of the methods for, and reliability of, deciding when the criminally insane can and should be allowed to reenter society. Read from cover to cover, this book is almost certain to clear up misunderstandings and shed new light on the ongoing controversy.

INSANITY AND THE LEGAL SYSTEM

n 1997, Dean Trammel, a student at Santa Monica Community College in California, boarded a US Airways jetliner in Los Angeles. During the cross-country flight to Baltimore, Trammel got up from his seat and began wandering the aisle. He tapped other passengers on the head with a pillow and blessed them. He announced that he was Jesus.

Trammel's behavior, annoying though perhaps also somewhat amusing, turned violent as the plane approached Baltimore. When the crew asked all passengers to take their seats in preparation for the landing, as regulations require, Trammel informed a flight attendant that God had told him to remain standing. A

A Park Police helicopter takes off outside the U.S. Capitol on July 24, 1998, after gunman Russell E. Weston Jr. stormed the building, killed two policemen, and wounded several tourists. Weston, who suffered from schizophrenia, claimed he was trying to save the world from cannibalism and disease. For centuries legal systems have struggled with what to do with mentally ill lawbreakers.

Andrew Goldstein in the custody of New York City police officers. Goldstein, who threw a woman in front of an oncoming subway train, later tried to mount an insanity defense.

crew member then ordered Trammel to sit down, but the young man didn't comply. Instead he grabbed a flight attendant and hurled her across two rows of seats. As four men moved to subdue him, Trammel flailed wildly and tried to bite them. They finally managed to restrain him using plastic handcuffs, a seat belt, and a necktie. Authorities arrested Trammel after the plane had landed safely in Baltimore.

At his 1999 trial for assault, Trammel's attorneys argued that the young man should not be held criminally responsible for his actions. One of the defense's expert witnesses, a psychiatrist, testified that Trammel had been diagnosed with manic depression (also called bipolar disorder) and that he had been in the midst of a "manic episode" during the Los Angeles–to–Baltimore flight. During such an episode a person afflicted with manic depression may experience delusions—persistent, false beliefs about oneself or other persons or objects.

Trammel's lawyers were relying on the insanity defense—a defense that, while it has a centuries-old pedigree in English and American law, remains controversial. They were arguing that their client's mental condition at the time of his crime precluded him from knowing right from wrong.

Statistically, criminal defendants rarely invoke the insanity defense, and when they do, it rarely succeeds in winning them acquittal. In addition, despite public perceptions to the contrary, most cases in which the insanity defense is offered—like Dean Trammel's—involve crimes other than homicide.

Yet it's hard to listen to the news or read a newspaper without coming upon a story in which someone accused of murder has, or claims to have, a mental illness. National headlines over a 12-month period include an April 1998 case in Delaware, in which a former auto worker shot a man to death and sexually assaulted the victim's wife for four days; the fatal shooting by a Montana man of two police officers at the United States Capitol in the summer of 1998; the stabbing murder of a pregnant woman by her fiancé in New York State in 1998; the January 1999 murder of a young woman, killed when a man pushed her into the path of an oncoming subway train in New York City; and an April 1999 shooting rampage by a 70-year-old man in a Salt Lake City library, which killed two people and wounded five.

Defense lawyers would argue that, because of mental illness or mental defect, the people accused of these crimes could not be judged by ordinary standards of guilt or innocence. Their mental condition interfered with their capacity to appreciate the difference between right and wrong. Or perhaps they knew that what they were

James Hadfield fires a pistol at King George III in the Drury Lane Theatre, May 15, 1800. At trial Hadfield's attorney, Thomas Erskine, successfully argued that his client should not be held responsible for the assassination attempt because he was delusional.

doing was wrong but because of their mental condition were unable to stop themselves. In either case, all of these killers mounted, or proposed to mount, an insanity defense. The goal of that legal strategy is to lead a jury to a verdict of "not guilty by reason of insanity."

The insanity defense is rooted in a basic principle of justice: that it is unfair to hold persons responsible for their actions when they don't know, or can't control, what they're doing. Of course, this is a very broad description of the ideal behind the insanity defense. In order to avoid abuses (for couldn't all suspects claim that they were unable to control themselves when committing a crime?), society has been searching for centuries for a way to measure insanity so that only the truly ill are spared criminal punishment.

The legal definition of insanity has varied throughout the years, from culture to culture, state to state—and even, at times, judge to judge. Among laypeople, the term *insane* is little understood and much abused. Even when someone behaves in an only slightly odd or unexpected way, others frequently say that he or she is "insane."

It's important to note that insanity isn't a psychiatric term at all. Professionals today who work with the mentally ill would never call their patients "insane" or, even worse, "crazy." These are generic, and even derogatory, terms. A mental health professional would instead provide a specific diagnosis, such as manic depression or paranoid schizophrenia.

Insanity is a legal concept, one whose definition has been shaped by lawmakers, judges, lawyers, and public opinion. Diagnosing a mental illness and measuring how an illness can affect a defendant's thinking, however, aren't easy.

Under ancient Hebraic law, lunatics (along with "idiots" and young children) were deemed incapable of distinguishing between good and evil or right and wrong. Thus they could not be held criminally responsible. In Anglo-Saxon culture, victims' families weren't allowed to take personal vengeance—which was normally their prerogative—if the perpetrator was considered insane or committed the crime by accident.

Henry de Bracton, a 13th-century legal scholar who wrote the first detailed description of English law, indicated that because children and madmen lacked guilty intent they could not be considered criminally liable. In the following centuries, various judges and legal sources came up with different ways to measure insanity, but the rules were inconsistently applied and sometimes little understood.

In the early 14th century, English law established that for someone to be found insane, that person's defenders had to show that his or her mental capacity was no better than that of a "wild beast." In the 16th century, a judge named Sir Anthony Fitzherbert described an "idiot" as someone "who cannot account or number twenty pence, nor can tell who was his father and mother, nor how old he is, etc." Such a person could not be held accountable for a crime. In the 17th century, insanity was defined as having "no free will," brought about by "a total defect of the understanding."

The trouble with all these tests, however, was that none seemed to capture the subtleties that might arise in a particular situation. Matthew Hale, a 17th-century legal commentator, thought it wrong to create a single test, yet he understood that juries needed some guidelines. He therefore suggested that in borderline cases the jury should consider whether the allegedly insane defendant had the understanding normally possessed by a child of 14. But this guide was considered impractical and was rarely used.

After James Hadfield tried to shoot King George III in 1800, Hadfield's defense attorney, Thomas Erskine, suggested another way to measure insanity. The presence of delusions, Erskine argued, should be sufficient to judge a defendant insane. The argument seemed appropriate because Hadfield's behavior did not match earlier measures of insanity.

Hadfield had fired a pistol at the king as he entered his box at the Drury Lane Theatre. The prosecution argued that Hadfield was not insane because he had clearly acted with reason and intelligence in the planning and execution of the crime. Prosecutors pointed out that Hadfield had been able to plan the shooting, go to the theater, select a seat with a view of the king's box, aim the gun, and pull the trigger.

Erskine countered that it was rare to find insane people who were so completely mad that they couldn't, for instance, find their way home or recognize their relatives. In fact, someone who was insane might be able to plan a crime and might even know the difference between right and wrong. What makes them insane, Erskine argued, is the presence of delusion. In Hadfield's case, delusions had dogged him for six years after he suffered severe war injuries. At first he imagined that he was King George. Later he thought he was speaking to God and Christ, and still later that he himself was God or Christ. He had arrived at the notion that humanity was doomed, and he wanted to die. But, not wanting to kill himself or King George, he contrived to feign an assassination attempt so that he would receive the death penalty.

When Erskine offered dozens of witnesses to detail Hadfield's mental history, the judge and the prosecutor agreed that the jury should be told to enter a verdict of not guilty according to the following explanation: "He being under the influence of Insanity at the time the act was committed."

Erskine had successfully used the insanity defense in the Hadfield case. Nevertheless, no clear definition of legal insanity yet existed in English law. As a result, there were no rules to guide judges and juries in future cases. This would eventually change during the middle of the 19th century following a famous legal case that involved an attempt on the life of Great Britain's prime minister.

THE M'NAGHTEN RULE

I n 1843, Daniel M'Naghten walked up to the home of British prime minister Robert Peel at 10 Downing Street in London. M'Naghten pulled out a gun and, in a case of mistaken identity, shot and killed Peel's secretary, Edward Drummond, instead of the prime minister.

What was the killer's motive? M'Naghten, a Scottish woodworker, thought that he was the target of a conspiracy hatched by the pope and the prime minister's Tory Party.

M'Naghten was arrested and put on trial—a trial that to this day stands as one of the most significant milestones in the history of the insanity defense. To the public, the case seemed cut-and-dried. After all, M'Naghten was caught red-handed murdering someone; therefore, people thought, he must be guilty.

An engraving depicting the trial of Daniel M'Naghten. The 1843 case remains one of the most important in the history of the insanity defense.

Sir Robert Peel, the Tory prime minister, was M'Naghten's target. In a case of mistaken identity, however, M'Naghten shot and killed Peel's secretary.

But M'Naghten's lawyer invoked the insanity defense, and its exact definition in English law was still not fixed. M'Naghten's lawyer, supported by the testimony of several doctors, said that the defendant was suffering from delusions that essentially made him incapable of distinguishing between right and wrong.

Three physicians testified that M'Naghten was insane. One of them, Dr. E. T. Monro, gave a detailed description of M'Naghten's thoughts: how he constantly observed people pointing at him, believed a shadowy crew followed him wherever he went, saw secret signs and signals all around him, was afraid to go out at night because he believed he would be assassinated, thought newspaper articles contained unflattering allusions to him, and believed that people were trying to poison him.

The other two doctors, in circumstances that we would find strange today, never examined M'Naghten but were merely spectators at the trial. They concluded that he was insane based on the testimony of witnesses and M'Naghten's behavior at the trial.

But the prosecution, taking an approach still common among prosecutors today in insanity trials, tried to show that the methodical way M'Naghten planned and carried out the crime proved that he was thinking rationally and therefore was not insane. The prosecutor pointed out that M'Naghten had been seen for about two weeks in the vicinity of the prime minister's residence. This, the prosecutor claimed, was a sign that he was carefully planning his crime. When asked why he was there during those two weeks, M'Naghten had made up stories, saying in one instance that he was waiting for someone, and on another occasion that he was a policeman. This demonstrated that he'd been sane enough to lie to avert suspicion, the prosecutor charged. The prosecution also called witnesses who knew M'Naghten. They said they'd never seen him behave oddly and that he seemed to conduct himself in an ordinary manner.

In the end, however, Chief Justice Nicholas Tindal, with the agreement of the prosecutor, decided to halt the trial, declare M'Naghten insane, and have him committed to an insane asylum. Tindal explained that he was particularly persuaded by the testimony of the two physicians who had never examined M'Naghten and "who are strangers to both sides and only observers of the case."

The public found the ruling outrageous. So did Queen Victoria. In fact, so great was the controversy that a panel of 15 judges was convened to develop a specific definition for the insanity defense.

Under their definition, called the M'Naghten Rule, a defendant is insane when he "was laboring under such a defect of reason, from disease of the mind, as not to know the nature and quality of the act he was doing; or, if he did know it, that he did not know he was doing what was wrong." The judges also addressed the issue of "partial insanity," a description that seemed to apply to M'Naghten's condition because he conducted himself normally most of the time even as he was dogged by paranoid delusions. The judges ruled that in such cases the court should base its verdict on the story presented in the defendant's delusions. In other words, if the defendant imagined that he was killing in self-defense, he should be acquitted because someone who actually killed in self-defense would be acquitted. On the other hand, if, according to the defendant's delusions, he killed for revenge—a motivation that wouldn't absolve him in any way of the crime—then he should be found guilty.

Only one member of the 15-judge panel offered a dissenting opinion. That judge argued that the panel's report was too vague and that there was probably no rule that could accommodate every possible trial involving an insanity claim. Despite that judge's dissent, the M'Naghten Rule, which is sometimes referred to as the "right-wrong test," became the guiding instruction to juries in insanity cases throughout the British Empire as well as in almost every state in the United States.

Over the years, jurisdictions have altered the definition. Some have narrowed it, while others have tried to expand it; still others have abandoned it outright. But today the M'Naghten Rule remains the basis for the insanity defense in about 15 U.S. states. The other states—except for Montana, Idaho, and Utah, which have so severely limited the insanity defense as to have

Queen Victoria was among the many Britons incensed at the outcome of the M'Naghten trial. In the wake of the controversy, a 15-judge panel was convened to establish a clear legal definition of insanity.

virtually abolished it—have adopted other, albeit similar, definitions of legal insanity.

The M'Naghten Rule filled a needed hole in the law because it offered a succinct and clear standard for determining who was legally insane and who was not. And yet ever since its formulation, certain groups have found the rule inadequate.

Many psychiatrists, for instance, found the right-wrong test far too restrictive. To them, a definition of insanity should include anyone mentally ill enough to be committed to an asylum, even though the vast majority of people placed in asylums could distinguish between right and wrong. Jurists, in response, argued that the rule was never meant to absolve all mentally ill people from guilt, but rather to determine who among the mentally ill could be held legally responsible for their actions.

In New Hampshire in the late 1860s, a psychiatrist, Dr. Isaac Ray, and a judge, Associate Justice Charles Doe, formulated perhaps the broadest definition of legal insanity: when the crime committed "was the offspring or product of mental disease in the defendant." Gone were the right-wrong test and knowledge of "the nature and quality of the act." This guideline, known as the New Hampshire Rule, has been in effect in that state ever since.

Doe felt strongly that the definition of insanity should not be restricted to a particular kind of mental illness. He and Ray hoped that other jurisdictions would adopt their definition of insanity, which was far broader than the M'Naghten Rule, but not until the 1950s did another court follow their lead.

Another attempt to broaden the M'Naghten Rule involved the introduction of the concept of "irresistible impulse." Under this formulation, someone who has knowledge of right and wrong should nonetheless be deemed insane if that person was compelled by an impulse beyond his or her control to commit a criminal act. Many people criticized this idea, noting that everybody at one time or another is subject to destructive impulses, and that the ability to resist such impulses is exactly what separates law-abiding citizens from criminals. Others noted that it was very difficult to determine which crimes were propelled by an irresistible impulse and which were not. In spite of these objections, by the beginning of the 20th century about half the states recognized irresistible impulse along with the M'Naghten Rule.

Judge David L. Bazelon (at left) broadened the federal courts' definition of insanity in his decision in the 1954 case Durham v. United States.

In 1954, the U.S. Court of Appeals for the District of Columbia adopted a variation of the New Hampshire Rule in a case called *Durham v. United States*. In his decision, Judge David L. Bazelon broadened the definition of the insanity defense from the M'Naghten right-wrong test to state that "an accused is not criminally responsible if his unlawful act was the product of mental disease or mental defect."

According to this rule, two conditions must be met to produce a verdict of not guilty by reason of insanity: first, the defendant must have a "mental disease or defect"; and second, the disease or defect must have caused him or her to commit the "unlawful act."

Ultimately, the ruling gave psychiatrists and experts testifying about a defendant's mental health a great deal of power. Since it was up to the experts to determine whether the defendant had a mental disease and whether the crime was "the product of" that disease, the jury's verdict would be little more than a validation of the experts' testimony. Of course, in cases involving the insanity defense, two sets of experts—one for the defense and one for the prosecution—typically present opposite conclusions.

Under the broadly worded Durham Rule, the frequency of "not guilty by reason of insanity" verdicts steadily rose, from 0.4 percent of cases in Washington's federal district court in 1954 to 14.4 percent of cases in 1961. Most other courts, however, found the rule too broad and did not adopt it.

In 1972, a new definition of insanity was hammered out by the American Law Institute (ALI). It said that "a person is not responsible for criminal conduct if at the time of such conduct as a result of mental disease or defect he lacks substantial capacity either to appreciate the criminality [wrongfulness] of his conduct or to conform his conduct to the requirements of law." This definition made it easier for a person to claim insanity than under the M'Naghten Rule; "appreciate" is not as strong as "know the nature and quality of the act" in M'Naghten. Thus under the ALI definition a person accused of a crime could be found "not guilty by reason of insanity" for no other reason than that he or she didn't have an appreciation of the wrongfulness of what he or she was doing. Almost half the states have adopted the ALI definition.

However, like previous attempts to define insanity under the law, the ALI definition strikes many people as inadequate. On the one hand, some psychiatrists and psychologists believe that even with its expanded scope, the definition excludes many defendants who are mentally ill at the time they commit a crime and who belong in asylums, not prisons. On the other hand, many laypeople object to any rule that seems to excuse criminal conduct.

At the heart of any legal definition of insanity is the issue of *mens rea*. This Latin term, meaning "guilty mind," refers to criminal intent—that is, the conscious decision to commit a crime. (Mens rea also includes recklessness.) Under the law, prosecutors must prove that a person accused of committing a crime possessed mens rea, a criminal state of mind. A person's actions may produce a great deal of harm, but they aren't considered criminal in the absence of the intent to do harm (or in the absence of a reckless disregard for the possibility that harm will be caused).

Consider the cases of two men who are each house-sitting for their girlfriend while she is away on vacation. The first man, angry at the way his girlfriend has been treating him and upset that she didn't ask him to go on the vacation, decides to teach her a lesson. He finds some gasoline in the garage, splashes it on the carpets and furniture, and ignites it with a match. The house burns down. The second man is watching late-night TV when he falls asleep on the sofa with a lit cigarette. Embers from the cigarette fall to the floor, where they set the carpet on fire. By the time he wakes up, the fire has spread, and he is lucky to escape with his life. The house, however, burns down.

Objectively speaking, each man has caused the same amount of harm: he has destroyed his girlfriend's house. But there is a huge moral difference between the two, and the law recognizes this. The first man will be charged with arson because he intended to burn down the house. The second man won't be charged, as the fire was an accident that resulted from carelessness rather than from any intent on his part to commit a crime.

In a case such as this, most people can readily understand and accept that the absence of mens rea, or criminal intent, makes all the difference. But the situation becomes a bit murkier in insanity cases when the harm done was not accidental. For example, in 1993 in Maine, a woman named Tonia Kigas starved to death her five-year-old daughter. Kigas withheld food from the girl for about five weeks. She did this, she told investigators, because God had commanded her to deliver the child, who was possessed by evil, back to him. The death of her daughter was the outcome Kigas wanted; in that sense the killing was completely intentional. Yet because of her delusions Kigas lacked the capacity to distinguish right from wrong and form criminal intent under the law, and she was found not guilty by reason of insanity.

Such outcomes are sometimes difficult for people to accept, and in general the public's perception of the insanity defense is negative. This has been especially true in the last 20 years in response to changes in the way the criminally insane are treated. In the past, those found not guilty by reason of insanity were often held in institutions for many years, or even a lifetime. In fact, many spent far more time locked away in mental institutions than they would have spent in prison had they been found guilty.

But over the last two decades, some insanity acquittees are finding themselves back on the streets much more quickly. That change, which has produced a public backlash, can largely be attributed to advances in psychiatric treatment. With medication, many patients can be restored to mental health. Court rulings also make it far more difficult to keep insanity acquittees confined in a hospital after they recover from mental illness. Once released, such people, because technically they have not committed a crime, have all the rights of ordinary citizens.

Adding to public disapproval of the insanity defense is a misperception that it is used far more often than is actually the case. One poll found a widespread though incorrect belief that all sorts of infamous criminals had successfully employed the defense. In fact, only about 1 percent of defendants invoke the insanity defense. And among those who do try to use it, no more than 1 in 5 beat the rap, and some studies show that as few as 1 in 20 do. What's more, the vast majority of insanity pleas, up to 70 percent, do not involve the charge of murder.

THE CASE
OF JOHN
HINCKLEY JR.

No case in recent history has had a more significant impact on the negative public perception of the insanity defense than the trial of John Hinckley Jr. Hinckley was found not guilty by reason of insanity in his attempt to kill President Ronald Reagan.

On March 30, 1981, at 2:25 P.M., Reagan had just finished a speech to union delegates at the Hilton Hotel in Washington, D.C. He was leaving the hotel and waving to the crowd.

"I didn't see him at first. I just saw Secret Service and the police," Hinckley said later. Hinckley was standing in the crowd, a .22-caliber pistol in his pocket.

Moments after John Hinckley squeezed off six shots at President Reagan, a Secret Service agent stands ready to provide cover while colleagues behind him mob the would-be assassin. The prone bodies in the foreground are policeman Thomas Delahanty and press secretary James Brady, both of whom were wounded in the attack.

"Then I saw him. He was . . . waving across the street first, then he turned toward us again, or was in the motion of turning. I never let him get all the way around. . . . That's when I pulled out the gun and started firing."

Hinckley fired six "Devastator" bullets, which are designed to explode on impact to cause maximum damage. The first shot hit Reagan's press secretary, James Brady, in the face. Hinckley's second shot hit policeman Thomas Delahanty in the back. The third went into a building across the street. The fourth hit Timothy McCarthy, a Secret Service agent, in the chest. The fifth slammed into the bulletproof glass of the president's limousine. The final shot ricocheted off the car, pierced Reagan's chest, and settled in a lung, just inches from the president's heart.

The shots were discharged in just a few seconds. A moment after it was over, a Secret Service agent brought Hinckley down. "As I was going through the air, I can still remember the gun going off and a desperate feeling of 'I have got to get to it. I have got to get to it and stop it,' " the agent said. "I came down on top of the assailant, with my right arm around his head. . . . He was still clicking the weapon."

None of the shots proved fatal, though James Brady suffered brain damage and was subsequently confined to a wheelchair. Reagan recovered fully.

The shooting took place in front of dozens of people, including reporters. The scene was captured on film and replayed countless times on national television. There was no question that Hinckley was the shooter.

Although Hinckley faced 13 criminal counts, including attempting to kill the president and assault with a deadly weapon, his attorneys tried to bargain. They offered prosecutors a plea of guilty in exchange for a recommendation that the sentences be served concurrently, amounting to a 15-year term, rather than consecutively, which would have meant life in prison.

The prosecution refused, so the trial moved forward. The defense then entered a plea of not guilty by reason of insanity.

The defense made its case carefully, building a detailed portrait of Hinckley's life. In April 1976, Hinckley had impulsively sold his car, dropped out of school at Texas Tech in Lubbock, Texas, and headed for Hollywood, where he imagined he would become famous as a singer or songwriter. He wrote to his parents about contacts he was making in the record business, but in fact there were no such contacts. Hinckley also told his parents about a girlfriend, Lynn Collins. He described vacations, visits, and breakups with Lynn, but this too was a complete fabrication. There was no Lynn Collins.

Jodie Foster (center) and Robert De Niro (right) in a scene from the 1976 motion picture Taxi Driver. *John Hinckley, who watched the movie more than a dozen times, apparently came to identify with Travis Bickle, the mentally unstable character played by De Niro. At the same time, Hinckley became obsessed with Foster.*

During this time Hinckley watched the movie *Taxi Driver* 15 times. Lynn Collins was based on Betsy, a character in the film. One of the experts for the defense, Dr. William Carpenter Jr., said that Hinckley had come to identify with the main character of *Taxi Driver*, Travis Bickle, a violent loner who works as a cabbie. In the film, Bickle pursues Betsy romantically, but when she rejects him, he decides to assassinate the presidential candidate for whom Betsy works. Bickle never gets close enough to the candidate to succeed, however. He then becomes interested in saving Iris, a 12-year-old prostitute played by Jodie Foster. At the end of the film, Bickle shoots Iris's pimp, the manager of the hotel where she works, and one of her customers. In a gesture that is meant to be triumphant, he raises a bloody finger to his temple, acting like a man who is going to shoot himself.

In March 1977, Hinckley returned to Lubbock, where he became interested in the American Nazis. "By the summer of 1978," he wrote in an autobiography for his psychiatrist, "at the age of 23, I was an all-out anti-Semite and white racialist." At 24, he created the American Front, which espoused racist views. He called himself national director and made up everything about the group, including a list of members from 37 states.

In May 1980, Hinckley read in *People* magazine that Jodie Foster was going to be attending Yale University, in New Haven, Connecticut, in the fall. In August, he made an agreement with his parents that he would try to get his life back on track and take a writing course at Yale.

In September, he left his parents' home in Denver and flew to New Haven. He never enrolled in the writing class, however. Instead, he was driven by a fantasy that Foster was being held captive at Yale and that he had to rescue her. Once rescued, she would fall in love with him and they would be happy forever. On September 20 and 22, he called Foster, but no relation-

A Polaroid self-portrait by John Hinckley. As his mental condition deteriorated, Hinckley contemplated suicide and the assassination of the president.

ship developed. In his autobiography he wrote: "My mind was on the breaking point. A relationship I had dreamed about went absolutely nowhere. My disillusionment with EVERYTHING was complete."

Hinckley decided he could gain Foster's attention and affection by shooting the president, who at the time was Jimmy Carter. Vincent Fuller, his attorney, characterized Hinckley's thinking this way: "The thought that by stalking the President of the United States, he could in some way establish a relationship with the young woman is bizarre."

Hinckley went to Dayton, Ohio, where Carter was making an appearance on October 2, but decided not to shoot the president there. On October 9, he went to Nashville, Tennessee, still on Carter's trail, but again decided not to shoot him. Hinckley crisscrossed the country several times, traveling between New York, New Haven, Denver, and other cities in what Fuller called an "absolutely absurd travel pattern" that was "irrational, purposeless, aimless." At the Nashville airport he was charged with a misdemeanor and fined $62.50 when airport security guards found three guns in his luggage. The cops kept his guns but let Hinckley go. Later that month he tried to kill himself with an overdose of pills.

In November, Hinckley sent the Federal Bureau of Investigation an anonymous letter: "There is a plot underway to abduct actress Jodie Foster from Yale University dorm in December or January. No ransom. She's being taken for romantic reasons. This is no joke! I don't wish to get further involved. Act as you wish."

Hinckley was profoundly disturbed by the killing of former Beatles member John Lennon on December 8, 1980, and went into what he called "deep mourning." In the coming months, Hinckley contemplated homicide and suicide. Meanwhile, he remained obsessed with Jodie Foster, putting notes, letters, and poems in her dorm mailbox, and sometimes even under her door.

In March, on the advice of a psychiatrist their son had seen for a few months, Hinckley's parents cut him off, saying they wouldn't give him money or let him return home. They hoped that this "tough love" approach would force him to get a job and put his life back on track. "That," defense attorney Fuller contended to the jury, "was the severance of his last anchor to reality."

On the day he shot the president, Hinckley just happened to notice Reagan's schedule in the *Washington Star*. He took some Valium, a powerful tranquilizer, and wrote a letter to Jodie Foster. In it he said, in part:

> As you will know by now, I love you very much. Over the past seven months, I've left you dozens of poems, letters and love messages in the faint hope that you could develop an interest in me. Although we talked on the

phone a couple of times I never had the nerve to simply approach you and introduce myself. Besides my shyness, I honestly did not wish to bother you with my constant presence. . . .

Jodie, I would abandon this idea of getting Reagan in a second if I could only win your heart and live out the rest of my life with you, whether it be in total obscurity or whatever.

I will admit to you that the reason I'm going ahead with this attempt now is because I just cannot wait any longer to impress you. I've got to do something now to make you understand, in no uncertain terms, that I am doing all this for your sake! By sacrificing my freedom and possibly my life, I hope to change your mind about me. This letter is being written only an hour before I leave for the Hilton Hotel. Jodie, I'm asking you to please look into your heart and at least give me the chance, with this historical deed, to gain your respect and love.

I love you forever,

John Hinckley

THE BATTLE
OF THE EXPERTS

There was little argument between the defense and the prosecution over the facts of the Hinckley case. But each side had a profoundly different interpretation of their meaning. The defense saw Hinckley's behavior as a sign of profound mental illness that absolved him of responsibility for the attempted assassination of President Reagan. The prosecution, on the other hand, acknowledged that Hinckley was troubled, but not to the extent that he couldn't control his actions.

The prosecution produced two expert witnesses, both psychologists. These experts testified that Hinckley was troubled and had what they called a "narcissistic personality disorder." But they did not feel that his mental disorder caused Hinckley to shoot the president. They testified that Hinckley was in complete control of himself and was aware of what he was doing.

The prosecution didn't deny that Hinckley was mentally unstable. What it argued was that his mental

41

Attorney Vincent Fuller, seen here leaving court, initially tried to arrange a plea agreement for his client John Hinckley. After federal prosecutors balked, Fuller mounted an insanity defense.

condition had no bearing on his behavior in this particular case.

"There is a whole spectrum of mental disorders," prosecutor Roger Adelman said in his closing argument. "There is a whole spectrum of physical disorders. If you have the sniffles and a head cold, that is one thing. If you have double pneumonia, you have trouble. I'm not trying to equate the two, but I'm trying to let you know, as the evidence shows, there is a considerable spectrum and . . . it is not evident that [Hinckley] had any serious mental disorder on that day."

The clash between experts, common at modern insanity defense trials, poses unique challenges for the jury. Both sides usually have knowledgeable, experienced, and highly credentialed specialists, yet these experts usually reach opposite conclusions. This underscores not only the limits of expert psychiatric testimony, but the limits of psychiatry itself. Psychiatry is not an exact science in the way chemistry or biology is. No one can actually enter a defendant's head and study its contents under a microscope. Instead, psychiatrists interview the defendant, often for dozens and dozens of hours over many days and weeks. (One psychiatrist for the prosecution, Dr. Sally Johnson, interviewed Hinckley almost every day for four months.) They try to learn as much about a defendant as they can, then they draw their conclusions. But there is always room for a wide variety of interpretations.

The Hinckley trial was no exception. What the defense saw as clear signs of mental illness, the prosecution believed was something else. The defense said Lynn

Collins, Hinckley's imaginary girlfriend, proved that Hinckley was delusional. Prosecutors, however, said Hinckley invented her to deliberately manipulate his parents, since he invariably asked for money whenever he mentioned her. A defense psychiatrist said Hinckley's attempts to court Jodie Foster were "bizarre" and "a sign of disordered thought." But Adelman said that mere "poor judgment" was behind Hinckley's actions.

According to the prosecution, all that mattered about Hinckley's mental health was his condition when he pulled the trigger of his .22-caliber gun. In essence, the prosecutor was suggesting that all the evidence detailing Hinckley's strange behavior in the months and years before the shooting was irrelevant.

"This indictment doesn't talk about anything else than March 30, 1981, or anything else that is depicted in this evidence," Adelman said in his closing argument. "He is not charged here with being sad at Christmas. . . . He is not even charged here with stalking President Carter in Nashville or President Carter out in Dayton. He is charged with 13 crimes that happened at 2:20 P.M. on the 30th of March."

But Hinckley's defense attorney disagreed. "Don't be misled by Mr. Adelman's suggestion that only March 30, 1981, should be considered," Vincent Fuller said. "It took years and years of growth of the disease or disorder to lead to the state of mind on March 30, 1981."

In his instructions to the jurors, Judge Barrington D. Parker explained that they must find Hinckley not guilty by reason of insanity if, as a result of mental disease or defect, Hinckley lacked "substantial capacity to either conform his conduct to the law or appreciate the wrongfulness of his conduct." And, under the American Law Institute test in federal court, the burden was on the government to prove beyond a reasonable doubt that the defendant was not insane (once enough evidence had been offered to raise the issue in the first place).

The jury reached its verdict on June 21, 1982, after four days of deliberation. It found that a reasonable doubt existed about Hinckley's sanity during the assassination attempt. It therefore found him not guilty by reason of insanity on all 13 counts. Some of the jurors interviewed after the verdict said that they were simply following the law and that the prosecution hadn't presented evidence strong enough to prove that Hinckley was sane.

The general reaction from the public was shock and outrage. People had seen the televised images of the shooting and Hinckley being brought to the ground by Secret Service agents. There was no question that he'd pulled the trigger. To many, the finding of not guilty by reason of insanity seemed like a legal loophole to get an obviously guilty man off the hook. What many people probably didn't realize was that the verdict did not make Hinckley a free man. He was committed to St. Elizabeth's Mental Hospital in Washington, D.C.

Hinckley himself only fanned the flames of controversy by calling up the *Washington Post* and saying, "I'm going to walk out the door whether the public likes it or not." (Nearly two decades after his acquittal, Hinckley remains locked away in a mental ward at St. Elizabeth's.)

In response to the public outcry, the U.S. Senate and House of Representatives held hearings on the insanity defense. In 1984, Congress passed the Insanity Defense Reform Act, which limited the use of the insanity defense. The act applied only to federal trials. It read in part: "It is an affirmative defense to a prosecution under any federal statute that, at the time of the commission of the acts constituting the offense, the defendant as a result of a severe mental disease or defect, was unable to appreciate the nature and the quality or the wrongfulness of his acts. Mental disease or defect does not otherwise constitute a defense."

This definition placed the burden of proof on the

defense, rather than the prosecution. Thus, it was now up to the defense in federal trials to prove with "clear and convincing evidence" that the defendant was insane. Unlike the American Law Institute definition, the new law also required that someone could be considered insane only if the mental disease was "severe." The statute replaced the ALI definition phrase "lacks substantial capacity to appreciate the criminality of his conduct" with "was unable to appreciate." Thus a defendant must have a total lack of understanding—rather than just partial comprehension—of his or her act to be considered insane.

The law also dealt with punishment. Recent developments in psychiatry had made it possible that a person found not guilty by reason of insanity would spend less time in a mental institution than that same person

Members of the jury that found John Hinckley not guilty by reason of insanity testify before the Senate Judiciary Committee's Criminal Law Subcommittee. Outrage at the Hinckley verdict spurred Congress to pass the Insanity Defense Reform Act, which limited the use of the insanity defense in federal trials.

would have spent behind prison bars if he or she had been found guilty of a crime. The new law permitted the period of incarceration to be extended to the maximum allowable for an actual crime, even if the person recovered from mental illness earlier.

In response to the Hinckley decision, many state legislatures passed laws giving juries the option of returning a new verdict: "guilty but mentally ill." To return this verdict, the jury must find two things: first, that the defendant committed the offense charged; and second, that while mentally ill, the defendant was not legally insane at the time he or she committed the offense. A defendant found guilty but mentally ill faces the same punishment as a defendant found guilty, and he or she will generally serve the sentence in prison, not at a mental institution.

Supporters have touted the guilty but mentally ill option as a way to accomplish several goals. First, they say, it removes a heavy burden from jurors. In the face of conflicting expert testimony, jurors often have a difficult time deciding whether a defendant really was insane, and thus not legally responsible, when he or she committed a crime. The guilty but mentally ill verdict constitutes a sort of compromise: jurors can acknowledge that a defendant was mentally ill, but they don't have to decide the much more difficult question of whether that mental illness was sufficient to absolve the defendant of responsibility. It also ensures that defendants who have committed violent crimes won't be quickly released back into society, which is a major concern not only of jurors but also of the public at large.

Critics charge that the guilty but mentally ill verdict is a sham. While jurors may believe that the verdict guarantees treatment for a defendant in prison, this is not necessarily the case. In fact, studies show that only about two-thirds of those found guilty but mentally ill ever receive any mental-health treatment in prison. And even when they do, the treatment is often inadequate. So in practice, a guilty verdict and a guilty but mentally ill verdict may amount to exactly the same thing. The trouble with this, argues Ralph Slovenko, a professor of law and psychiatry at Wayne State University Law School in Detroit, is that "jury deliberation gives meaning to society's ideas of personal responsibility or irresponsibility. By substituting guilty but mentally ill for the old insanity plea, this function is lost, and jurors can avoid the moral issues inherent in deciding guilt or innocence."

Many observers believe that reducing the number of insanity acquittals was the clear purpose of legislators who enacted laws permitting the guilty but mentally ill verdict. If that is indeed the case, the results have been mixed. In Georgia, for example, the number of acquittals has dropped. In Michigan, which led the way in adopting the new verdict, there has been no change.

Nevertheless, studies do show that defendants found guilty but mentally ill spend more time incarcerated than those who successfully use the insanity defense. The new laws, along with the more restricted definition of insanity, have had a major impact on the American legal system and the trials of defendants accused of committing murder or other violent crimes.

WHO IS INSANE?

On May 20, 1998, Kipland Kinkel was sent home from his high school in Springfield, Oregon, in the custody of his father because he had brought a weapon to school. At the house, the 15-year-old shot his father in the back of the head, killing him. Then Kinkel waited for his mother to arrive home from her job as a teacher and murdered her as well.

At 8 A.M. the following day, Kinkel—armed with two pistols and a semiautomatic rifle—returned to Thurston High School, went to the cafeteria, and opened fire on his classmates. The young gunman killed 2 and wounded more than 20 before several students wrestled him to the ground as he tried to reload.

After being taken into custody, Kinkel, who had been prescribed the antidepressant Prozac, claimed he heard voices inside his head. And those voices, he said, had driven him to kill. "I have to kill people," he wrote. "I don't know why. I am so sorry."

At his trial in 1999, Kinkel's lawyers planned to have him enter a plea of not guilty by reason of insanity. Later Kinkel decided to plead guilty. This would avoid a trial, and he might also receive a shorter sentence from a judge. Nevertheless, he was eventually sentenced to more than 100 years behind bars.

Was Kinkel really insane? The experts disagreed. Dr. Park Dietz, an eminent forensic psychiatrist who examined Kinkel, conceded that the youth suffered from depression. Kinkel had also been fascinated with guns and explosives, and his father had bought him a pistol. But, according to Dietz, "we've got thousands of cases of people with more warning signs than Kip Kinkel who didn't do anything." Dr. William Sack, a child psychiatrist, took a different view. Sack said that Kinkel had visions and heard voices. One of them belittled Kinkel, and the other told him to commit murder. Sack believed that Kinkel suffered from schizophrenia.

Schizophrenia, which afflicts about 1 percent of the population, is the most common form of psychosis, or severe mental disorder characterized by loss of touch with reality. The thoughts of schizophrenics tend to lack coherence or logical connections, and their emotional responses to situations seem inappropriate and are often extremely muted, as though they had no feelings. Schizophrenics frequently experience delusions and hallucinations, sensory perceptions of things that have no existence in reality. Among those who suffer from a prevalent form of the illness called paranoid schizophrenia, auditory hallucinations—such as hearing voices inside one's head—are particularly common.

Many people who have committed crimes and are found not guilty by reason of insanity suffer from schizophrenia. It is important to note, however, that most schizophrenics aren't violent.

The brains of some schizophrenics have abnormal appearances when viewed on a three-dimensional X ray, called a CAT scan. Dr. David Bear, who testified at

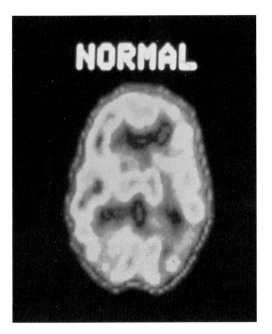 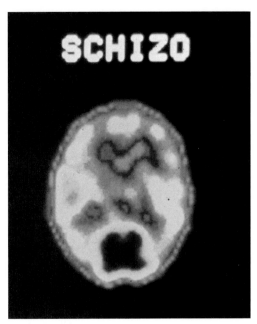

the trial of John Hinckley, believes that CAT scans may offer powerful evidence to help courts decide the crucial question in insanity cases: was the person actually responsible for his or her criminal behavior?

Dr. Stephen Lally, a forensic psychologist who examines people accused of committing crimes, believes that in general the question of whether a person is responsible can readily be answered by looking at the details of the crime and examining the perpetrator. "Usually I have little difficulty in deciding whether an accused individual qualifies for the insanity defense," Lally wrote in an article for the *Washington Post*. By way of illustration, he described the case of a homeless man who had attacked someone on the street during the middle of the day, within sight of a group of policemen. From his examination, Lally concluded that the man had long been afflicted by schizophrenia and believed that his victim was going to harm him. He was also incapable of appreciating that what he was doing was wrong or of controlling himself. "Oddly enough," Lally wrote, "the shorthand often used by experts to assess

Scans of a normal brain (left) and the brain of a schizophrenic. Some experts have suggested that brain scans might provide concrete scientific evidence of mental illness in insanity defense cases, thus replacing the subjective opinions of psychiatrists.

whether an individual's control is impaired is to ask whether he would commit the act with a policeman at his elbow. The homeless man did just that. He was, quite appropriately, found not guilty by reason of insanity and committed to [a] hospital."

Lally contrasted the case of the homeless man to that of Jeffrey Dahmer. Dahmer, a confessed serial killer from Milwaukee, Wisconsin, murdered 17 young men and boys, all but one of them between 1987 and 1991. Dahmer had drilled holes in the heads of some victims—while they were alive—in an effort to create zombies who would be his lifelong companions. After he killed his victims, he had sexual contact with their bodies, boiled them in a vat and ate parts, stored their skulls in a refrigerator, and collected bones for a "temple" that he believed would give him power. His behavior was so bizarre, so obviously abnormal, that many people assumed that Dahmer was insane. According to Dr. Lally, however, Dahmer "did not meet the threshold of having a serious mental illness; he hid his victims' bodies, showing that he was aware his behavior was wrong; when a police officer confronted him, he was able to control his actions."

Not every expert agreed with Lally's conclusions. At trial, Dahmer's lawyers offered an insanity defense and presented several witnesses who testified that the defendant's compulsions and delusions made him either incapable of following the law or unable to distinguish between right and wrong. (Under Wisconsin law, the burden of proof was on the defense.)

Dr. Fred Berlin, director of the Sexual Disorders Clinic at Johns Hopkins University, testified that at the time of the murders, Dahmer had been unable to conform his conduct to the law because he suffered from necrophilia, a mental disorder characterized by the desire to have sex with corpses. In Dahmer's case, Berlin argued, that desire was overwhelming; it was like "a cancer of the mind."

Another defense witness, forensic psychiatrist Dr. Carl Wahlstrom, testified that Dahmer had "bizarre and delusional ideas." His attempts to create zombies who would function as his personal companions, and his belief that he could use victims' body parts to construct a power-bestowing temple, Wahlstrom argued, were indicative of psychosis.

Expert witnesses for the prosecution disagreed. Dr. Park Dietz did not believe that Dahmer suffered from a mental disease or defect at the time he committed the murders. His desire for sex with the dead was obviously indicative of an abnormal mind, but like everyone else, Dietz said, Dahmer had been free to choose whether or not to act on that desire.

This was a point driven home by District Attorney E. Michael McCann, who argued that the defendant had simply given in to selfish impulses. Dahmer,

Jeffrey Dahmer sits between his lawyers in court. Experts are divided on whether serial killers like Dahmer fit the legal definition of insanity.

McCann said, "knew exactly what he was doing every step of the way" and was "able to turn his urges on and off as easily as a light switch." He'd turned them off when it had been necessary to avoid detection—for example, when two police officers showed up at his apartment after one of his victims, dazed and bleeding from a head wound, had escaped. Dahmer somehow managed to convince the cops that he and the victim—a Laotian immigrant who didn't speak much English—had just had a lovers' quarrel. Tragically, the officers returned the boy to Dahmer's apartment, and shortly after they left Dahmer killed him.

In the end, the jury may have been most persuaded to reject Dahmer's insanity claim by the testimony of two court-appointed psychiatrists. Both characterized the defendant as a deeply disturbed individual, but both denied that his mental condition rose to the level of insanity in the legal sense. Dahmer was found guilty and sentenced to 15 life terms. In 1994 he was murdered in prison by another inmate.

In some ways the question of whether serial killers like Jeffrey Dahmer should be considered insane reflects the difficulties and concerns with the insanity defense as a whole. Serial killers constitute only a small percentage of the people who commit murder, yet arguably they are society's most dangerous members. They do not kill for the reasons that motivate most murderers: anger, jealousy, greed. Rather, their motives are wholly psychological. Serial killers derive emotional satisfaction from the act of killing itself, along with the rituals they create to precede and follow the murder, such as finding and subduing a victim and using mementos of the crime to relive the thrill.

Obviously by any ordinary measure, the behavior of all serial killers manifests a severe mental defect. And indeed, many serial killers have offered insanity defenses. But some experts maintain that by legal standards, serial killers aren't insane. "Serial killers . . . all make choices," says John Douglas, former head of the FBI's behavioral profiling unit and a pioneer in the study of serial murderers. "We can debate and ponder whether they understood the morality of their choices, that murky right-or-wrong issue. But I can't imagine many instances in which, for example, a violent criminal bludgeons an elderly woman with a pick ax without understanding that he's causing her to die." Most serial killers, experts believe, perceive reality clearly, but they feel no moral or social obligations. Their only concern is personal gratification, which they find in killing others. "Serial killers know what they're doing," Douglas says. "They don't accidentally kill people. They don't have a problem understanding what death means, and that they have the power to kill. That's what excites them—the act of frightening, controlling, hurting, dominating and ultimately, in a few minutes or days, killing their victims."

Others aren't so categorical as Douglas. Robert Ressler, also a former FBI agent and pioneer in the field of behavioral profiling, believes that the mental disorders of some serial killers do rise to the level of legal insanity. For example, Ressler interviewed Jeffrey Dahmer for two days and concluded that "his compulsions and fantasies had taken over his rational mind. . . . There was no way to view this tormented man as having been sane at the time of his crimes."

Unlike serial killers such as Jeffrey Dahmer, John C. Salvi III seemed to be on a mission. On December 30, 1994, Salvi attacked two abortion clinics in Brookline, Massachusetts. He killed two women, Shannon Lowney and Lee Ann Nichols. He shot Nichols 10 times, shouting: "This is what you get! You should pray the rosary!"

After the murders, Salvi fled the area and headed south. But his rampage had not ended. He attacked another abortion clinic in Norfolk, Virginia, where he was finally captured.

Bailiffs carry John Salvi III out of the courtroom after an outburst during his trial for the murder of two women at an abortion clinic. The jury rejected Salvi's insanity defense, finding him guilty. He was sentenced to life in prison without parole.

Salvi's lawyers decided to use an insanity defense to keep their client out of prison and secure treatment for him. Several experts testified that he was suffering from schizophrenia. Indeed, they questioned whether Salvi was even mentally competent to stand trial. Under the law, a defendant cannot be tried if he is incapable of understanding what the proceedings are about and unable to assist in his legal defense. A defendant who is judged mentally incompetent must receive treatment until such time as the court believes he is fully aware of the legal process. Despite the opinions of several defense experts, however, Salvi was considered competent to stand trial.

In trying to convince the jury that his client was insane, one of Salvi's attorneys, J. W. Carney Jr., characterized him as a "sick, sick young man." Severe

mental illness, Carney claimed, had led Salvi to commit murder.

The prosecution disagreed, saying that Salvi was
fully responsible for his criminal conduct. As evidence
of the defendant's sanity, prosecutors cited Salvi's careful planning of the attacks as well as his flight to Virginia to avoid arrest. John Kivlan, an assistant district
attorney, branded him nothing more than a terrorist.

The jury agreed, finding Salvi guilty of murder. He
was sentenced to life in prison with no possibility of
parole. He later committed suicide in prison.

As with other high-profile insanity defense trials,
the outcome of the Salvi case prompted criticism.
Unlike the Hinckley case, however, this time the criticism came from people who thought the appropriate
verdict was indeed not guilty by reason of insanity.
"Jurors have been to some extent brainwashed by the
media that there's something wrong with having a crazy
person found not guilty," Boston attorney Norman
Zalkind said. "There are people that really aren't
responsible for what they do. I think Salvi was one."
Jack Levin, director of the Program for the Study of
Violence and Conflict at Northeastern University,
agreed. "Jurors feel the same way the public feels; that
is, any murderer who pleads NGI [not guilty by reason
of insanity] will get off, will serve a short sentence in an
institution for the criminally insane, and will get out."

Some experts believe that a harsh attitude toward
the criminally insane arises from a more general get-
tough approach toward criminals of all kinds. This
approach, which emphasizes severe punishment for
lawbreakers, has recurred periodically throughout
American history. Alternating with it have been periods during which the rehabilitative ideal prevailed.
During these periods, crime was often blamed on social
conditions such as poverty, and it was believed that
criminals could be rehabilitated with proper treatment.

The most recent get-tough trend began during the

and sending the matter back to the lower court for reconsideration. Writing for the appeals court, Judge David S. Tatel said:

> A jury listening to a non-delusional Weston explain, perhaps quite passively, that at the time of the crime he believed he had to save the world from the Ruby Satellite System will be considerably more skeptical than a jury that sees and hears the person Dr. Johnson saw and heard: Russell Weston, delusional and unmedicated, explaining in the present tense that there is a "Ruby Satellite System" and that he, in fact, went to the Capitol in search of the override console to save the country from "human corpses rotting, turning black, and spreading the most deadliest disease known to mankind."

The appeals court's ruling made it possible that Weston would never stand trial for the Capitol shootings because he would never be mentally competent.

A defendant's strange behavior in front of the jury—which Weston's lawyers hoped would help them make their case for insanity in the event their client ever came to trial—was on display at the 1997 trial of another schizophrenic charged with murder. Though a multimillionaire and, in fact, the wealthiest murder defendant in American history, John E. du Pont showed up every day for his trial in the same old blue sweatshirt. Whether this represented a conscious effort on the part of the defendant or his lawyers to sway the jury, or whether it was merely a manifestation of du Pont's mental illness, is unknown.

Du Pont, an heir to the fortune of a corporation that manufactures chemicals and synthetic fibers, had been a patron of elite wrestlers. On his southeastern Pennsylvania estate, Foxcatcher Farm, he constructed an elaborate training facility for Olympic hopefuls in the sport. Several wrestlers lived on the estate's grounds with their families. One of them was David Schultz, who had won a gold medal at the 1992 Summer Olympics and had set his sights on the 1996 Summer

Games in Atlanta.

On January 26, 1996, the 57-year-old du Pont drove his car to Schultz's house on the Foxcatcher estate. According to witnesses, Schultz greeted his patron in the driveway. "Hi, coach," he said. In response du Pont pulled out a gun and shot the wrestler three times. As Schultz lay dying, du Pont was heard to say, "You have a problem with me?" Following the killing, du Pont fled the scene and holed up in his house, where he held off police for two days before being captured.

Du Pont's defense attorneys pled their client not guilty by reason of insanity. Thomas Bergstrom, du Pont's lawyer, noted that the multimillionaire suffered from schizophrenia. "This is about a killing for no reason whatsoever by a man who suffered from a mental disease that took away his ability to know what he did was wrong," Bergstrom told the jury. Psychologists who examined du Pont and testified in his defense said that he believed Schultz was part of an international gang that had sworn to murder him. Du Pont, who at times imagined that Nazis were spying on him and that insects had invaded his body, was also afraid his home was about to be attacked. The millionaire had been seen driving a tank around his farm. According to defense psychologists, he believed that someone else—someone who looked like him and belonged to a splinter group of the Buddhist religion—had actually killed Schultz.

Olympic gold medalist David Schultz. In January 1996 Schultz was shot to death by his wealthy patron, John du Pont, on the grounds of du Pont's estate.

John du Pont's unkempt physical appearance may have been a manifestation of mental illness—or a conscious attempt to influence the jury.

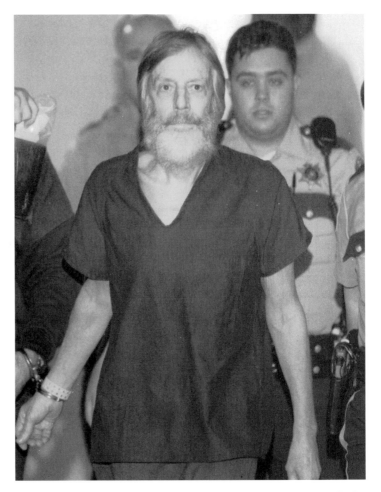

Schultz's widow also testified for the defense. "[H]e hallucinates, he talks about things that he hears and sees," she said of du Pont. "The last year he's been consistently under the impression that he is the Dalai Lama [the spiritual head of Tibetan Buddhists] and usually dresses in all red."

The prosecution, however, presented an entirely different picture of du Pont. Assistant District Attorney Joseph McGettigan claimed that du Pont was angry at Schultz for maintaining a friendship with another wrestler whom du Pont had driven off his estate at gunpoint. Du Pont also believed that Schultz was trying to ruin his reputation in the wrestling community, the assistant D.A. said. McGettigan further suggested that du Pont believed himself above the law because of his wealth and power. "I could get away with murder if I wanted," the multimillionaire had earlier remarked.

In addition, as is often the case in insanity-defense trials, the prosecution cited the defendant's postcrime behavior as evidence that he was not insane. Not only had du Pont fled the crime scene and taken refuge in his house, but during the two-day standoff with police, he asked negotiators more than 100 times to contact his personal lawyer. These are the actions, McGettigan said, of a sane man.

In the end, however, the jury gave neither the prosecution nor the defense the verdict it wanted. Instead of finding the defendant not guilty by reason of insanity or convicting him of first-degree murder, jurors delivered a verdict of guilty but mentally ill, convicting the multimillionaire of the lesser crime of third-degree murder. Du Pont was sent to a state psychiatric hospital to be treated for his illness and confined for his crime.

The jury's verdict in the du Pont case may be seen as an attempt to recognize gradations of guilt in a mentally ill defendant. While du Pont's mental state may not have totally absolved him of responsibility for the crime, in the jury's mind it did make a conviction for first-degree murder inappropriate.

Likewise, some jurisdictions formally recognize a state of mind between the all-or-nothing legal extremes of insanity on one hand and full responsibility on the other. Diminished capacity, closely related to but not synonymous with the insanity defense, allows a defendant to be charged with a lesser degree of offense, or to receive less severe punishment, based on an impaired mental condition that falls short of insanity. The legal principle has figured prominently in a number of controversial trials, including the recent case of an infamous bomber.

THE UNABOMBER: A CASE OF DIMINISHED CAPACITY?

On June 10, 1980, a book arrived at the offices of Percy Wood, the president of United Airlines. It had been sent to Wood by someone signing himself Enoch W. Fisher. Unbeknownst to the recipient, the book contained a bomb. When Wood opened it, the bomb exploded, injuring him.

The FBI linked the incident with two previous bombings. In the first, which occurred in May 1978, a package bomb exploded in a parking lot at the University of Illinois at Chicago, injuring one person. In the second, a bomb exploded in the cargo hold of an American Airlines plane in 1979; although no one was killed, the pilots had to make an emergency landing. The FBI decided to open a new file on the bomber, calling it UNABOM, for university and airlines bombings. The unknown person who had sent the bomb—and who, over the next 15 years, would continue to send package bombs targeting corporate executives, computer and high-tech workers and researchers, and academics—

65

became known as the Unabomber.

In 1981 a bomb discovered outside the computer room at the University of Utah was safely destroyed with no injuries or loss of life. The following year, however, two package bombs sent to universities exploded. One, addressed to a professor at Vanderbilt University in Tennessee, injured the secretary who opened it. The other injured a professor of electrical engineering and computer science at the University of California at Berkeley.

After a hiatus of nearly three years, the Unabomber returned with a vengeance, sending four bombs in 1985. The first, which again targeted Berkeley, seriously injured a graduate student in the computer area in May. The second, mailed a month later to Boeing, an aircraft manufacturer in Washington State, was safely disarmed. In November, the Unabomber sent his third bomb of the year to a University of Michigan professor. It injured two persons. FBI agents noted that the Unabomber seemed to be getting better at his craft: each bomb was more powerful than the previous one.

The fourth bomb of 1985, which exploded on December 11, finally claimed a life. The victim was Hugh Scrutton, the owner of a computer store in Sacramento, California.

In early 1987, a witness spotted the Unabomber planting a bomb in a computer store in Salt Lake City, Utah. The police sketch depicted a curly-haired man with a mustache, wearing a hooded sweatshirt and aviator sunglasses. Perhaps because he had finally been spotted and feared capture, the bomber went into retirement for more than six years.

He resumed his bombing spree in June 1993, striking twice over a three-day period. On the 22nd, a package bomb injured Dr. Charles Epstein, a geneticist at the University of California at San Francisco. On the 24th, the target was David Gelernter, a professor of computer science at Yale University, who sustained serious injuries in the Unabomber attack.

That same year, the Unabomber finally tried to communicate his motives for killing and maiming his victims. In a letter to the *New York Times*, he outlined his anti-industrial, anti-high-tech philosophy. Not only was the environment being destroyed, he said, but computers were leading humanity to the brink of disaster.

In 1994 the Unabomber killed again. This time the victim was Thomas Mosser, an advertising executive who opened a deadly package bomb addressed to him at his home in New Jersey.

In April 1995 the bomber claimed his final victim. Gilbert Murray, the president of the California Forestry Association, was killed by an exploding parcel at his office in Sacramento.

Later that year, the Unabomber sent a rambling 35,000-word statement to the *New York Times* and the *Washington Post*. The manifesto, titled "Industrial Society and Its Future," detailed the bomber's beliefs about the dangers of technology. "The technophiles," it said, "are taking us all on an utterly reckless ride into the unknown. Many people understand something of what technological progress is doing to us yet take a passive attitude toward it because they think it is inevitable. But we . . . don't think it is inevitable. We think it can be stopped. . . . Until the industrial system has been thoroughly wrecked, the destruction of that system must be the revolutionaries' ONLY goal."

The Unabomber told the newspapers that he would stop his serial bombings if they printed his manifesto in full. The editors of the two papers were understandably reluctant to provide a forum for a terrorist who had killed 3 persons and wounded 23. However, the FBI believed that if the manifesto were published, a reader might recognize the writer's words and tip off law enforcement. On September 19, 1995, the *Times* and the *Post* jointly printed the Unabomber's tract.

The tactic worked. A man named David Kaczynski

contacted the FBI and told agents that the Unabomber manifesto closely resembled letters written by his brother, Theodore. After putting Ted Kaczynski under surveillance and gathering evidence, the FBI arrested him in early 1996 at his cabin in a remote area of Montana. Materials taken from the cabin, including a diary, seemed to link Kaczynski to the bombing spree.

By all accounts Ted Kaczynski was a highly intelligent, even brilliant, man. He had graduated from Harvard University and later taught mathematics at the University of California. In 1969 he'd left the university, eventually moving into the Montana cabin. But intelligence and mental stability are two different matters, and with piles of incriminating evidence arrayed against their client, Kaczynski's lawyers contemplated an insanity defense.

However, Kaczynski himself believed that he was quite sane. He had undertaken the bombing campaign and written the manifesto to draw attention to—and ultimately help stop—what he saw as dangerous advances in technology. Now he feared that no one would take his ideas seriously if everyone thought he was mentally ill. In papers found at his cabin, Kaczynski had emphasized that he did not want to be seen as "a sickie." Nevertheless, his lawyers decided to have him examined by psychiatrists. He agreed to the examination only to prove to them—and everyone else—that he was not insane.

One psychiatrist, David Foster, met several times with Kaczynski and concluded that he was suffering from paranoid schizophrenia. "Mr. Kaczynski chronically views accidental or intentional personal contact with other people, newspaper articles, scientific advances, commercial and residential development, air traffic, and radio and television broadcasts as threats to his survival," Dr. Foster concluded. The psychiatrist added that Kaczynski's fear of being labeled mentally ill was in fact further evidence that he suffered from men-

Theodore Kaczynski during his days as a mathematics professor at the University of California at Berkeley.

tal illness. Another specialist who examined Kaczynski reported that tests of his brain showed an abnormal condition that exists in people suffering from schizophrenia.

The government lawyers prosecuting Kaczynski disagreed with these findings. They wanted the defendant examined by their own experts, but he refused. People who knew Kaczynski in Montana also seemed to believe he was completely sane. In his book *The United States of America Versus Theodore John Kaczynski,* author Michael Mello quotes a man named Chris Waits, who said he knew Kaczynski very well in Montana. "I've never seen anyone more sane than Ted," Waits said. "He's calculating beyond description." Another point Mello notes—and one that prosecutors would be sure to emphasize—was how careful and methodical Kaczynski had been over the course of his long bombing campaign. He'd managed to elude law enforcement, including the FBI, for 17 years. This was not the work of an insane person, Mello concludes, echoing an old argument.

One of the Unabomber's victims, Professor Gelernter of Yale, suggested that Kaczynski was not insane but evil. "A lot of people in this country have a predisposition to believe that if you kill people with bombs, you must be insane," Gelernter said. "We know that's not true. We know sane men are capable of arbitrary bestiality."

In the end, Kaczynski's lawyers concluded that they could never successfully mount an insanity defense, particularly given their client's unwillingness to consider this option. They decided instead to offer a defense of "diminished capacity." If successful, this defense would lead not to an acquittal but to a trial on lesser charges and hence a reduced sentence. The best they could hope for, Kaczynski's attorneys felt, would be to avoid the death penalty for their client.

Essentially the diminished capacity defense recognizes that, because of trauma, mental impairment or disease, or even intoxication, some defendants are incapable of possessing the mental state necessary to be held responsible for a specific crime. Unlike the insanity defense, a diminished capacity plea doesn't assert that the defendant is *totally* without responsibility for his or her criminal actions. Rather, it suggests that because of his or her mental state the defendant should be held *less* responsible.

Consider charges that would cover homicide. The most serious crime, first-degree murder, involves causing the death of another person intentionally and with premeditation. The lesser crime of second-degree murder involves causing the death of a person intentionally but without premeditation. Second-degree manslaughter, less serious than second-degree murder but still a crime, is defined as causing the death of a person recklessly—that is, without premeditation or intent.

Federal prosecutors wanted to try Ted Kaczynski on the charge of first-degree murder, and they intended to seek the death penalty. In resorting to a diminished capacity defense, Kaczynski's lawyers hoped to convince the jury that, while their client's bombings had been intentional, his mental impairment precluded him from being able to premeditate killing his victims, an element required for the prosecution's charge of first-degree murder. This defense would shift the burden of proof to the prosecution, which would have to demonstrate that Kaczynski sent the bombs with the clear intent of taking lives. With luck, defense attorneys might get their client convicted of second-degree murder and sentenced to life imprisonment.

Diminished capacity pleas, which only a minority of states currently permit, have a decades-long history. Like the insanity defense, diminished capacity is controversial, both among legal professionals and the general public. This is due in large measure to the perception that this defense has been used to subvert justice in several high-profile cases.

No case is more prominent in this regard than *California v. White*, the 1979 murder trial of a former San Francisco city supervisor. So widespread was outrage at the verdict that it would be no exaggeration to call the case the John Hinckley of diminished capacity defenses.

In 1978, after the enactment of a gay-rights bill he opposed, Dan White had resigned his seat on San Francisco's board of supervisors. Soon afterward, however, White reconsidered his decision and tried to get Mayor George Moscone to reinstate him. Moscone refused.

On November 27, 1978, White—armed with a handgun and carrying extra bullets— crawled through a basement window into San Francisco's city hall to avoid metal detectors at the entrances. Evading Moscone's bodyguard, White found the mayor in his office and emptied his nine-shot pistol into Moscone's body. The mayor died in the attack. After reloading his

San Francisco mayor George Moscone (right) and city supervisor Harvey Milk during the signing of a gay-rights bill, 1977. After former city supervisor Dan White murdered the two men, his attorneys presented a successful—and extremely controversial—diminished capacity defense that the press dubbed the "Twinkie defense."

gun, White walked across city hall to find Harvey Milk, an openly homosexual city supervisor and a political opponent of his. He discharged another nine bullets at Milk, killing him as well.

The facts of the case seemed to support a first-degree murder conviction. It was hard not to see a high level of premeditation, and malice, in White's actions: avoiding metal detectors, bringing extra ammunition, pumping nine shots into each of his victims.

Yet at trial his attorney mounted a diminished capacity defense. Martin Blinder, a psychiatrist for the defense, testified that White suffered from untreated depression. Evidence of this depression, Dr. Blinder said, could be found in the defendant's eating habits: formerly athletic and health-conscious, White had been living on junk food, including Hostess Twinkies, before the killings. The psychiatrist also suggested, parenthetically, that the sugar from all the junk food might have worsened a chemical imbalance in White's brain.

Because of his depression, the defense argued, White was incapable of premeditating the killings. Thus he couldn't be found guilty of first-degree murder.

To the surprise of almost everyone, the jury accepted the diminished capacity defense, finding White guilty of two counts of voluntary manslaughter, the least serious offense jurors could have chosen. White's sentence, seven years and eight months, struck many observers as gallingly light for a double murderer.

The controversy was compounded by inaccurate reporting in the media. A host of news stories derided what was dubbed the "Twinkie defense," making it sound as if White's lawyer had argued that the junk food he'd eaten *caused* him to commit the killings. In fact, the defense had never put forward that proposition. Aside from a single offhand comment from Dr. Blinder, the defense hadn't even suggested that the junk food contributed to the crime. Rather, the defense's case rested on the contention that White suffered from depression and that this lessened his culpability. Whatever the actual merits of that argument, chances are that most people would have found it less difficult to swallow than the Twinkie defense. However, in the face of public pressure, California's legislature moved to abolish the diminished capacity defense.

Another controversial defense based on the concept of diminished capacity has been called "black rage." This defense can be traced to a case in Long Island, New York. In 1993 Colin Ferguson, a black man, went on a shooting rampage on a rush-hour commuter train. He killed 6 passengers and wounded 19 others.

Ferguson's attorney, the renowned defense lawyer William Kunstler, tried to offer a diminished capacity defense based on the defendant's exposure to society's racism and discrimination against blacks. This, Kunstler claimed, had filled Ferguson with an uncontrollable

Colin Ferguson, charged in a deadly shooting spree on a Long Island commuter train, rejected a "black rage" defense, dismissed his lawyer, and acted as his own counsel. Despite the testimony of many eyewitnesses, he argued that a white man had actually been the shooter. Many trial observers believed that Ferguson's bizarre courtroom behavior was evidence of severe mental illness.

rage, which boiled over on the commuter train.

Other defendants have since offered similar "black rage" defenses, but in the end Ferguson did not. He fired Kunstler and acted as his own lawyer. Though observers thought his behavior at trial was bizarre, Ferguson didn't present an insanity defense. Instead, in a rambling presentation to the jury, he claimed that he hadn't actually been the shooter, despite scores of eyewitnesses who testified to the contrary. The real killer, he maintained, was a white man who had stolen his gun from a bag under his seat after Ferguson had fallen asleep. The jury was not convinced. It found him guilty of murder. When he came before the judge for sentencing, Ferguson tried to claim that he was like John the Baptist from the New Testament, being persecuted unjustly. The judge, however, called Ferguson "selfish" and a "coward" and sentenced him to life in prison for his crimes.

A diminished capacity defense that is less controversial than black rage or the so-called Twinkie defense has been offered by women who have killed their abusive partners. Psychologists have identified a condition called battered-woman syndrome, which some consider a form of post-traumatic stress disorder. Battered-woman syndrome, which occurs after repeated physical abuse at the hands of a husband or boyfriend, may be characterized by a state of psychological paralysis in which a woman believes that the abuser is all-powerful and that she cannot get away from him. In addition, a battered woman may have a distorted perception of the actual danger to her life posed by her partner.

Defense lawyers have used expert testimony on battered-woman syndrome to explain why their abused clients didn't simply leave the abusive partner—and in some cases, to explain why they killed the partner in the absence of immediate physical danger. The psychological effects of repeated abuse, it has been argued, alter the way a victim thinks, reacts, and behaves, diminishing her capacity to form criminal intent. Although a diminished capacity defense based on battered-woman syndrome is by no means accepted by every jurisdiction or jury, some women accused of killing their partners have successfully used it. They have been charged with lesser offenses or have received reduced sentences.

Despite many instances in which the diminished capacity defense has been successfully used, Theodore Kaczynski, the accused Unabomber, didn't want to offer that defense. Though diminished capacity is not insanity, Kaczynski believed that such a plea would lead people to question his mental stability and therefore to dismiss his ideas.

However, his lawyers intended to use a diminished capacity defense, although they may not have made this illness.

March 5, 1997, to Sowards and Holdman: "Your approach is this: You put a shrink or two on the stand to 'tell my story,' you expose publicly all the most intimate details of my life, and then you ask the jury to take pity on me because I've had it so tough.

"I'm not going to let you take this approach."

Accused Unabomber Theodore Kaczynski (opposite page) feared that any suggestion he was mentally unbalanced would undermine his message. Above: Part of a note Kaczynski passed to his attorneys during a hearing, making it clear that he wouldn't countenance a diminished capacity defense.

clear to him. In November 1997, Kaczynski appeared in court in Sacramento with his lawyers. Jury selection was beginning for Kaczynski's trial. Defense attorneys and prosecutors began arguing over the tests of Kaczynski's mental condition, and whether prosecution psychiatrists should be allowed to examine him. Kaczynski became upset during the debate and, as the *New York Times* reported on November 25, "threw his pen across the defense table" in disgust.

A few days later, Kaczynski wrote a letter to the presiding judge in his case, Garland E. Burrell. "I unexpectedly learned for the first time in this courtroom that my attorneys deceived me," Kaczynski said. "In particular, I was led to believe that I would not be portrayed as mentally ill without my consent. But last Tuesday I learned that I had indeed been portrayed as mentally ill without my consent."

Outside the courtroom, newspapers had begun printing stories calling into question the Unabomber's mental stability. They quoted one of the defense psychologists, Karen Bronk Froming, as saying, "Mr. Kaczynski's superior intellect should not be confused with sound mental health." Meanwhile, a television

news program reported that Kaczynski's attorneys had filed "papers claiming he suffers from paranoid schizophrenia" and quoted one mental health expert as saying that Kaczynski believed he was "controlled by an omnipotent organization."

With the controversy swirling, Judge Burrell met with Kaczynski and his lawyers to discuss what defense approach should be used during the trial. Finally, they reached a compromise. Kaczynski's attorneys agreed not to use a mental defect or diminished capacity defense during the guilt phase of the trial. Kaczynski agreed that if he was found guilty, his lawyers could use such a defense during the sentencing phase, in the hope of avoiding a death sentence.

While the disagreement between defendant and counsel appeared to have been worked out, in fact it wasn't. Kaczynski's attorneys believed that it was in the best interest of their client to introduce the issue of his mental condition. Otherwise, it was very likely that he'd be found guilty of three counts of first-degree murder and sentenced to death. Although they had agreed not to offer expert testimony from psychiatrists to support a mental defect or diminished capacity plea, Kaczynski's attorneys decided to present nonexpert testimony and evidence to suggest that the defendant might be suffering from mental illness. As author Michael Mello points out, they could, for example, "show the jury photographs of Kaczynski 'before and after' he became a recluse hermit in the wilds of Montana." These pictures might indicate that his mental state had declined, and the jury might come to the conclusion that Kaczynski was suffering from mental illness.

Kaczynski had been declared mentally competent to stand trial and participate in his own defense. He believed that, since his lawyers were there to represent him, he had a right to determine what kind of defense they should present. And when he discovered what they intended to do, he wanted to fire them and represent himself.

However, Judge Burrell ruled that, with the trial about to begin, it was too late for Kaczynski to make that decision. Because the case could not be conducted the way he wanted, Kaczynski decided to plead guilty to murder. In return, prosecutors agreed not to insist on the death penalty. Kaczynski was sentenced to life in prison.

Critics such as author Michael Mello have argued that Judge Burrell erred in not permitting Kaczynski to defend himself. He was, after all, declared competent to stand trial. He should have been allowed to guide his own defense, the critics say. He should not have had to accept the legal strategy his attorneys devised if he disagreed with it.

Other observers argue that Kaczynski's lawyers were doing what was in his best interest—namely, constructing a defense that would give him the best chance of avoiding the death penalty. According to these observers, the evidence suggests that Kaczynski suffered from some form of mental illness or impairment. He may even have been a paranoid schizophrenic.

Did the Unabomber's crimes result from mental illness? Or was he simply evil? Should he have been held less responsible, or did he deserve to face charges of first-degree murder? As with the insanity defense in general, the Unabomber case produced no consensus and no easy answers.

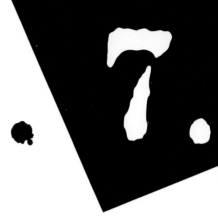

WHEN SHOULD THEY WALK THE STREETS AGAIN?

Insanity acquittees who have committed violent acts are likely to spend years locked away in mental institutions. Still, even those responsible for multiple murders may be released when doctors deem them cured—sometimes with tragic results.

In 1981, Margaret Nolan informed her husband that she wanted to divorce him and marry another man. She also wanted custody of their four-year-old child. Robert Nolan became so enraged that he killed his wife with a hunting knife—stabbing her 17 times and slashing her throat. He also murdered Margaret's boyfriend.

A jury later found Nolan not guilty because of mental illness. Although he was sent to a mental hospital, Nolan remained there only a few months before doctors, deciding that he was no longer a danger to himself or other people, released him.

Eventually Nolan remarried. Once again, the union came to a bloody end. After nine years of marriage, his second wife, Kimberly, decided that she wanted a divorce. Nolan again became murderously violent, this time using a shotgun. After he had killed Kimberly, Nolan turned the gun on himself.

Cases like that of Robert Nolan raise perplexing

questions regarding the final outcome of a successful insanity defense: When is it safe to let someone committed to a mental hospital for a violent crime back onto the streets? How should release decisions be made, and by whom? Isn't there always an element of guesswork involved in evaluating a person's mental health?

The stakes are quite high, of course. Prematurely releasing someone who is mentally ill and violent can have tragic consequences, as Robert Nolan demonstrated. Yet frequently a person's mental condition is no easier to assess in an institution than at a criminal trial. Indeed, even the American Psychiatric Association has conceded that it is very difficult for psychiatrists to accurately predict "long-term dangerousness." In other words, trained professionals cannot guarantee that a freed mentally ill killer won't kill again, even after he or she has received mental health treatment and appears sane.

To deal with this situation, some states have set up review boards to take ultimate responsibility for deciding when a person who has successfully made an insanity plea should be released and under what conditions. In Connecticut, for example, review boards are responsible for insanity acquittees for the same length of time that the acquittees would have spent in prison had they been convicted. Insanity acquittees are committed to high-security mental hospitals where the average length of stay is 27 years. Before individuals can be released, they must have a hearing or trial to determine whether they are still dangerous. Some people found not guilty by reason of insanity spend the rest of their lives institutionalized.

The nation's most famous insanity acquittee, John Hinckley, has remained at St. Elizabeth's Hospital in Washington, D.C., since 1982, a year after trying to assassinate President Ronald Reagan. At first, Hinckley didn't seem to respond to treatment and made several attempts to take his own life. "For years we were struggling and hoping for something to happen to John," said his father. "Around the beginning of [the 1990s], he just seemed to be coming out of it." Doctors stopped his medication in 1992. He was given a regular job at the hospital and permission to walk the grounds. Recent examinations indicate that he no longer suffers from serious mental illness. In 1999, the United States Justice Department decided to support a decision by federal judges that Hinckley be allowed to make visits outside the hospital grounds. "The John Hinckley of [the past] does not exist today," his mother has stated. Still, authorities are not yet ready to release Hinckley and return him to society.

The question of whether a criminal can safely return to the streets has been raised time and time again in one of the most bizarre cases in New York history: that of an immigrant dubbed the Staten Island Ferryboat Slasher. Juan Gonzalez, the admitted slasher, grew up in Cuba, where he worked as a farmer. In 1977 Gonzalez, together with seven other refugees fleeing the island's Communist regime, boarded a rowboat and headed for the Florida Keys. They landed on U.S. soil on March 19.

At first Gonzalez lived with his cousin Wilfredo in Miami. But he soon moved north to Elizabeth, New Jersey, where a job awaited him. There he began living with another cousin, Timetheo Infante.

In the fall of 1977, Gonzalez was arrested by police in New York City for gambling violations. He paid a fine and was released. Over the next decade or so, he was repeatedly picked up for similar minor infractions, but there is no indication that he was involved in serious crime.

In early July 1986, Gonzalez was living at the Fort Washington Armory shelter for homeless men in the Bronx, New York. After threatening people at the shelter, he was sent to Columbia Presbyterian Hospital. Records show that he displayed symptoms of paranoid

"[N]o Constitutional basis [exists] for confining [mentally ill] persons involuntarily if they are dangerous to no one and can safely live in freedom," Justice Potter Stewart wrote in the Supreme Court's O'Connor v. Donaldson decision. The 1975 decision made it more difficult to hold mental patients against their will.

schizophrenia and received treatment in the emergency room on July 3. Two days later, however, he was released.

Twenty-five years earlier, a patient like Juan Gonzalez might have been sent to a psychiatric ward for an extended period, even though he hadn't committed a crime. In previous times people deemed mentally ill could be institutionalized against their will much more readily. Little more than the subjective opinion of a psychiatrist—in some cases, in conjunction with the wishes of family members—often sufficed to take away a person's freedom. And once institutionalized, many patients confronted a catch-22 situation that made their release extremely difficult to obtain: disagreeing with a psychiatrist's assessment of their mental condition could be seen as evidence of mental illness, yet conceding that they were mentally ill meant remaining incarcerated to receive treatment. Furthermore, conditions in many of the nation's mental institutions were appalling.

In response to abuses in the system, advocates for the mentally ill pressed for, and won, sweeping changes. A series of court cases sharply restricted the use of involuntary civil commitment—that is, the commitment of noncriminal mental patients against their will. The United States Supreme Court declared, in the 1967 case *Specht v. Patterson*, that "involuntary commitment to a mental hospital, like confinement of an individual for any reason, is a deprivation of liberty which the State cannot accomplish without due process of law." Eight years later, in *O'Connor v. Donaldson*, the Court gave the states further direction in dealing with the mentally ill. "[T]he mere presence of mental illness does not disqualify a person from preferring his home . . . to an institution," the Court said. Furthermore, the Court ruled, "no Constitutional basis [exists] for confining such persons involuntarily if they are dangerous to no one and can safely live in freedom."

The standard that emerged was that unless a person with a mental illness presents an imminent danger to himself or herself or to others, that person cannot be held against his or her will. Thus, when doctors at Columbia Presbyterian Hospital believed that Juan Gonzalez was no longer an immediate threat to anyone, they had little choice but to release him.

On Sunday, July 6, 1986, a day after his release, Gonzalez rode the ferry that carried commuters between Manhattan and Staten Island. Later he would say that God had told him to throw rocks into the water that day and to return the following day to kill.

On Monday morning, July 7, Gonzalez boarded the ferryboat *Samuel I. Newhouse*. The ferry left Manhattan at 8:30 A.M. carrying about 500 passengers. Gonzalez had managed to smuggle on board a samurai sword with a 24-inch blade, which he had concealed in newspapers.

Lower Manhattan as seen from the Staten Island ferry. A day after being released from Columbia Presbyterian Hospital, where he had been treated for symptoms of schizophrenia, Juan Gonzalez rode this ferry and, he believed, received instructions from God.

"He was sitting in the middle deck, left side, toward the front when he started slashing people," acting police commissioner Richard Condon explained. "Then he went upstairs and started slashing people there." Two passengers died, and nine others were wounded. The dead included 65-year-old Rose Cammarota, who was making a regular visit to a close friend confined to a Staten Island nursing home. Stabbed repeatedly, Cammarota died on the boat. The other fatality, 61-year-old Jordan Walker, was also stabbed many times. In the midst of the attack, Walker suffered a heart attack and died.

Gonzalez might have claimed many more victims had he not been stopped by a retired police officer, Edward del Pino. Returning home after working all night as a security guard at an insurance company, del Pino saw people running from the area where Gonzalez was slashing with his sword. He later explained that he witnessed Gonzalez "lunging down repeatedly . . . stabbing a woman over and over. It was horrible." Del Pino pulled out the revolver he carried at his security job and told Gonzalez to put down the sword. When the slasher didn't respond, del Pino fired a shot and Gonzalez hit the deck to protect himself. Del Pino then ordered him to push the sword away and remain stationary. "I told him, 'If you move, you're dead,'" del Pino said.

When taken into custody, Gonzalez said that the "Father, Son, and Holy Spirit told me to do it." He was later examined by psychiatrists, who declared him mentally unfit to stand trial. The psychiatric report stated that Gonzalez "lacks the capacity through mental disease and defect to understand the proceedings against him and assist in his defense. . . . It is doubtful whether he could establish a working relationship with defense [attorneys] . . . [and he is] not fit to proceed."

Michael Bousquet, the assistant district attorney, challenged the psychiatric report. Bousquet asked that prosecution psychiatrists be permitted to examine Gonzalez. At a special hearing before Judge Norman Felig, the assistant district attorney's request was granted. After he heard the judge's decision, Gonzalez, who was present in the courtroom, declared, "My father said you're all going to die."

The two psychiatrists selected by the district attorney's office thoroughly evaluated Gonzalez and confirmed the earlier report. "His judgment is so impaired," one of the experts said, "that it is impossible for him to choose defense alternatives and strategy as may be advised by his attorney." As a result, Gonzalez was committed to a state mental hospital to be treated until he was considered mentally competent to stand trial.

The treatment continued until early 1988, when Gonzalez was found capable of participating in his own trial. His lawyer, William M. Frederick, decided that there was only one way he could successfully defend his client. "We're putting in an insanity defense," Frederick said.

Before the trial began, however, Gonzalez decided to plead guilty to killing two passengers on board the ferryboat and stabbing nine others. Nevertheless, Gonzalez claimed that he was not responsible for what had happened because of "mental disease and defect." The prosecution decided not to challenge the plea because it seemed clear from all the psychiatric reports that Gonzalez was suffering from paranoid schizophrenia at the time of the crime. He was placed in a secure mental health facility where he could receive treatment for his illness. One of the doctors who examined Gonzalez said that he suffered from a severe mental illness that had originated in adolescence, if not earlier. He experienced hallucinations in which God told him to kill his enemies.

After remaining in treatment for two years, Gonzalez asked to be moved to a less secure facility. Following a hearing that involved testimony from seven psychiatrists, the request was turned down. Under state law, however, Gonzalez had the right to appeal this decision at a hearing in front of a jury. After listening to expert witnesses from both sides, the jury decided that Gonzalez's condition had improved enough for him to be moved to a less secure psychiatric center. There he would be allowed to leave periodically, but only if accompanied by a member of the staff. In 1994, Gonzalez asked to be released from this center, but his request was denied. He remained under treatment and continued to be locked away from society.

In 1997, Gonzalez's doctors believed that his condition had improved so much that he was now ready to make periodic trips, or furloughs, away from the psychiatric center without being supervised. The district attorney's office disagreed, blocking the unsupervised furloughs. Once again, Gonzalez requested a jury trial. This time the jury decided that he should be com-

Juan Gonzalez, the Staten Island Ferry Slasher. Eleven years after his rampage, a jury decided that Gonzalez no longer presented a threat and should be released from the mental hospital where he had been held. A state supreme court justice blocked the release, but ultimately Gonzalez was granted unsupervised weekend furloughs—a frightening prospect for many New Yorkers.

pletely freed from the psychiatric hospital. Gonzalez's doctors believed that he was sufficiently better to no longer pose a threat to himself and to society, as long as he took the proper medication.

"I am stunned," said Assistant District Attorney Michael Bousquet. Relatives of the two people Gonzalez killed reacted just as strongly. "He is a mass murderer who killed two and maimed nine and now he's walking out the door? It's outrageous," said Roger Lee, the nephew of Rose Cammarota. Lee emphasized that Gonzalez had been locked up and treated at a hospital two days before he committed the murders in 1986. He feared that Gonzalez might kill again if allowed to return to society.

One local political leader added, "Mr. Gonzalez had to be heavily medicated to ensure that his psychotic outbursts could be controlled. If Mr. Gonzalez is now released, there will be no effective way to monitor his medication. This should send a shiver down the spine of every Staten Island Ferry rider."

Was this simply political rhetoric? Or did it express the views of many people in the community, worried that a mentally ill killer might never be well enough to be released without causing a threat to society?

Justice Michael DeMarco of the New York State Supreme Court apparently believed that Gonzalez was not ready to walk the streets again. DeMarco ordered a new trial. Until that time, Gonzalez was required to remain at the psychiatric center.

Before the trial could occur, however, Gonzalez's legal team and prosecution lawyers worked out a deal. Under the arrangement, concluded in 1999, Gonzalez was allowed to begin monthly unsupervised furloughs. "This is the safest way to go for the public," said Michael Bousquet. "The reason we agreed to this is because the case is ready to be tried. We believe a second jury would release him. We're following the recommendation of all the doctors—including our own."

The agreement called for Gonzalez to be given a two-hour pass each week. The length of the passes would gradually increase until Gonzalez was permitted to spend both days each weekend away from the psychiatric facility. Finally, if no incidents occurred, he would be fully released.

The case of Juan Gonzalez, like a long line of cases before it, crystallizes the concerns many citizens have with the insanity defense. It's important to remember the limited scope of the insanity defense in the American criminal justice system: the defense is infrequently invoked and even more infrequently successful; plus, in the majority of insanity defense cases the defendant is charged with a crime other than murder. Still, enough Juan Gonzalezes periodically emerge to give citizens pause. While few would argue that someone who truly cannot understand right from wrong should be punished, the question of how to measure insanity defies easy answers. And most everyone agrees that society must be protected from the violent mentally ill. Ultimately, the quest to be fair to the mentally ill while still affording innocent citizens sufficient protection involves a calculated risk. Only time will tell whether an insanity acquittee like Juan Gonzalez is truly ready to return to society.

Bibliography

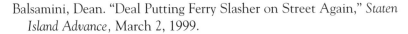

Balsamini, Dean. "Deal Putting Ferry Slasher on Street Again," *Staten Island Advance*, March 2, 1999.

Barnes, Julian. "Insanity Defense Fails for Man Who Threw Woman Onto Track," *New York Times*, March 23, 2000.

Booth, William. "Kaczynski Resists the Insanity Defense," *Washington Post*, December 26, 1997.

Fields-Meyer, Thomas, and Giovanna Breu. "By Reason of Insanity," *People*, September 1, 1997.

Glaberson, William. "Unabom Trial May Prove Landmark on Illness Plea," *New York Times*, December 9, 1997.

Goldberg, Debbie. "John du Pont Found Guilty, Mentally Ill," *Washington Post*, February 26, 1997.

Lally, Stephen. "Drawing a Clear Line Between Criminals and the Criminally Insane," *Washington Post*, November 23, 1997.

Mello, Michael. *The United States of America Versus Theodore John Kaczynski*. New York: Context Books, 1999.

Moran, Richard. *Knowing Right from Wrong: The Insanity Defense of Daniel McNaughton*. New York: The Free Press, 1981.

Palma, Leslie. "Cuban Slash Suspect Has Puzzling History," *Staten Island Advance*, July 9, 1986.

Palma, Leslie; Rochelle Bozman; and Jean Levine. "Ferryboat Slasher: God Told Me to Do It," *Staten Island Advance*, July 8, 1986.

Rohde, David. "For Retrial, Subway Defendant Goes Off Medication," *New York Times*, February 23, 2000.

Simon, Rita J., and David E. Aaronson. *The Insanity Defense: A Critical Assessment of Law and Policy in the Post-Hinckley Era*. New York: Praeger, 1988.

Vatz, Richard, and Lee Weinberg. "The Insanity Defense: Unconscionable Impact on Victims of Violence," *USA Today Magazine*, May 1998.

Verhovek, Sam Howe. "Teen-Ager Pleads Guilty in School Shooting," *New York Times*, September 25, 1999.

Wittek, Raymond. "Ferry Slasher Declared Competent for Trial," *Staten Island Advance*, March 4, 1988.

_____. "Ferry Slasher Pleads Guilty," *Staten Island Advance*, June 17, 1988.

Websites

"The Finding of Criminal Insanity."
http://www.cco.caltech.edu/~paulvig/Insanity.html

"The Insanity Defense."
http://www.psych.org/public_info/INSANI~1.HTM

"The Insanity Defense and Diminished Capacity."
http://www.law.cornell.edu/unabom

"The Trial of John W. Hinckley, Jr."
http://www.law.umkc.edu/faculty/projects/ftrials/hinckley/ACCOUNT.H TM

Index

Index

Index

Index

Picture Credits

RICHARD WORTH has 30 years of experience as a writer, trainer, and video producer. He has written more than 25 books, including *The Four Levers of Corporate Change*, a best-selling business book. Many of his books are for young adults, on topics that include family living, foreign affairs, biography, and history. He has also written an eight-part radio series on New York mayor Fiorello LaGuardia, which aired on National Public Radio. He presents writing and public speaking seminars for corporate executives.

AUSTIN SARAT is William Nelson Cromwell Professor of Jurisprudence and Political Science at Amherst College, where he also chairs the Department of Law, Jurisprudence and Social Thought. Professor Sarat is the author or editor of 23 books and numerous scholarly articles. Among his books are *Law's Violence*, *Sitting in Judgment: Sentencing the White Collar Criminal*, and *Justice and Injustice in Law and Legal Theory*. He has received many academic awards and held several prestigious fellowships. In addition, he is a nationally recognized teacher and educator whose teaching has been featured in the *New York Times*, on the *Today* show, and on National Public Radio's *Fresh Air*.